FOOD

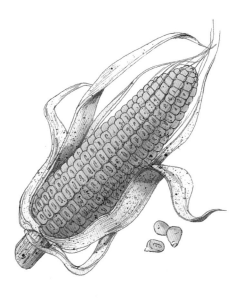

written by Dene Schofield *and* Charlotte Evans
illustrated by Studio Boni/Galante

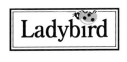

Ladybird

CONTENTS

WHY DO WE EAT?

We eat when we are hungry because food is a necessity of life. Food acts as our fuel, and so gives us the **energy** we need to carry out our lives. It also provides us with the materials for the growth, repair and general health of our bodies. Without enough food, we would be tired, weak and unhappy.

A balanced diet

The variety of food we need every day to keep us fit and healthy is shown here. A balanced **diet** includes fruit, vegetables, fish, **cereals** and milk products.

WHAT IS FOOD MADE OF?

Food is made up of five main groups of **nutrients**: proteins, carbohydrates, fats, **vitamins** and minerals. We should eat a variety of food to make sure our diet contains all the nutrients. We also need water.

Proteins
Proteins are used to build and repair our bodies. Meat, fish, milk, beans and cereals are good sources of protein.

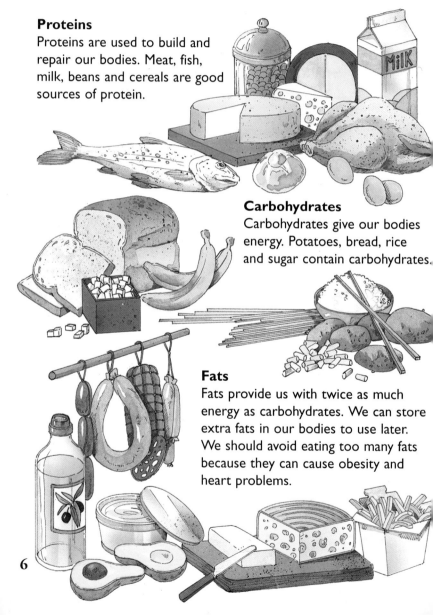

Carbohydrates
Carbohydrates give our bodies energy. Potatoes, bread, rice and sugar contain carbohydrates.

Fats
Fats provide us with twice as much energy as carbohydrates. We can store extra fats in our bodies to use later. We should avoid eating too many fats because they can cause obesity and heart problems.

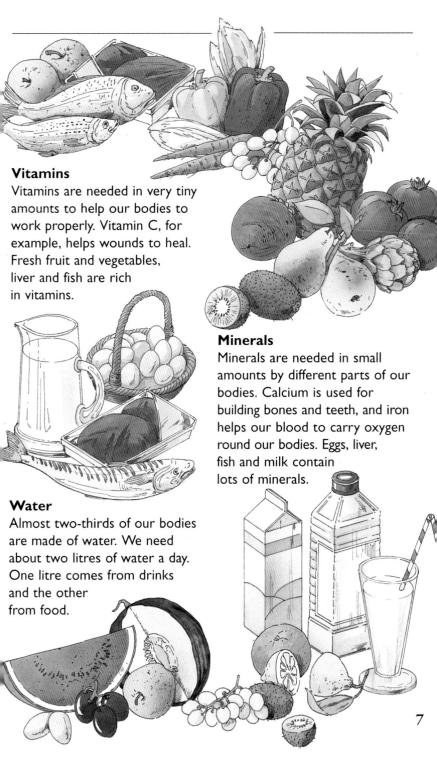

Vitamins

Vitamins are needed in very tiny amounts to help our bodies to work properly. Vitamin C, for example, helps wounds to heal. Fresh fruit and vegetables, liver and fish are rich in vitamins.

Minerals

Minerals are needed in small amounts by different parts of our bodies. Calcium is used for building bones and teeth, and iron helps our blood to carry oxygen round our bodies. Eggs, liver, fish and milk contain lots of minerals.

Water

Almost two-thirds of our bodies are made of water. We need about two litres of water a day. One litre comes from drinks and the other from food.

OUR STAPLE FOODS

Staple foods form a large part of our diet and we eat them every day. In many places they are made from types of grasses that have been grown since prehistoric times, and that we now know as cereals. The seeds we eat are called **grains**. They mostly contain carbohydrates.

Wheat

This is grown all over the world. It is usually ground into flour, which is used for making bread. Pasta and noodles are also made from wheat flour.

Millet and sorghum

These are important cereal crops in Africa because they grow quickly in hot, dry climates. They are ground to make flour for porridge or bread.

Rye

This grows in cold climates like Scandinavia and Russia where other cereals will not survive. It is made into flour which produces a dark and heavy bread.

Rice

Rice grows best in warmer parts of the world. It is an important staple food in Indonesia, India, China and other countries in Asia.

Over half the people in the world eat rice at every meal. Most rice is grown in flooded fields, called rice paddies, and is often sown and picked by hand.

Oats

Oats grow in cool climates and are eaten as porridge in many parts of Northern Europe.

Maize

One type of maize produces the head of seeds that we know as sweetcorn, or corn on the cob. The other, which has more starchy grains, is a staple food in East Africa, where it is ground and made into porridge. In Mexico and South America, the ground corn is used to produce a flat, pancake-like bread called a tortilla.

MEAT

Animals like chickens, cows, pigs, sheep, goats and rabbits are kept on farms for their meat, milk and eggs. Over many years animals have been specially **bred** to produce more milk or leaner, less fatty meat.

Pigs

Pigs are kept by farmers almost all over the world, although in some areas, such as the Middle East, pork is not eaten for religious reasons. Most parts of a pig can be eaten, including its feet or 'trotters'. Smoked or salted pork meat is called bacon or ham. Pigs are easy to feed – they eat almost anything.

Sheep

Sheep can live happily in hilly areas as they eat short, tough grass. Meat from adult sheep is called mutton. Meat from young sheep is called lamb.

Cows

Cattle are farmed on grasslands in many areas of the world. In some countries cattle are injected with drugs to produce more meat, as well as being fattened by grazing. Most male calves are reared for meat. Herds of female dairy cows are kept by some farmers to supply milk.

Geese

Geese are kept in flocks in China, providing plenty of meat and large eggs. Geese make excellent guards as they hiss loudly if anyone approaches.

Ducks

Ducks are a popular food in China, where large flocks are kept on rough pasture land. Many different parts of the duck, including the feet, liver and fat, are eaten.

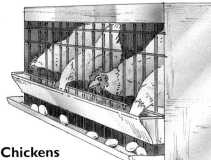

Chickens

Battery chickens are kept in large sheds in small wire cages with very little room to move. Free range chickens live outdoors in plenty of open space.

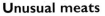

Unusual meats

In some areas of the world, a variety of animals are kept to be eaten. For example, snakes and frogs are a delicacy in China, and snails in France. Ostriches are now farmed in many countries.

FOOD FROM PLANTS

All fruit and vegetables come from plants. Fruit and vegetables contain vitamins and minerals and lots of **fibre**. Fibre is important in our diet as it helps us to get rid of waste from our bodies.

Vegetables

We eat many parts of vegetable plants, such as the leaves of cabbages, the roots of carrots, the flowers of cauliflower and broccoli, the stems of celery and the seeds of peas and beans. The potato is a swollen stem which grows underground, known as a **tuber**. Yams and sweet potatoes are also tubers.

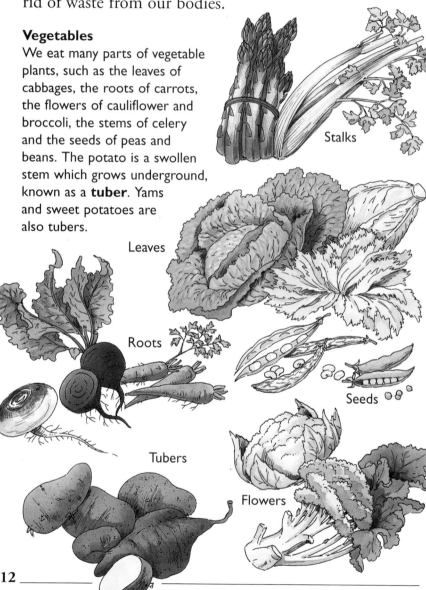

Stalks

Leaves

Roots

Seeds

Tubers

Flowers

Fruits

Fruits are juicy foods which contain the seeds of plants. There are a huge variety of fruits available, and they can be eaten raw, cooked or dried. They can also be crushed or squeezed into juices.

SEEDS

Many fruits contain seeds or pips. Tomatoes are often called vegetables but in fact they are fruits because they have seeds inside. The seeds of many other fruits are edible, such as pomegranates, kiwifruit and strawberries.

FOOD FROM THE SEA

There is an enormous variety of fish and shellfish found in the sea, and these have traditionally been used as food for thousands of years.

Fish for healthy eating
Fish is a healthy part of our diet because it contains proteins, vitamins and minerals, and is low in fat.

Fishing
A fishing trawler drags a huge, bag-like net behind it in the sea. Weights keep the mouth of the net open, trapping fish. Large fishing industries provide fish to feed lots of people. The biggest fishing nations are Japan, Russia and China. Recently, international laws have been passed to prevent overfishing our seas.

Shellfish
Crabs, prawns, scallops and mussels are collectively called shellfish. They have a hard, outer cover that has to be removed to reach the tasty food inside.

Seaweed
Seaweed is a popular food in many parts of the world. In Japan it is dried in the Sun before being sold in flat sheets, shredded into strips or ground into powder.

Fish fingers
Most fish fingers are made from a large fish called cod. The flesh is cut up into strips, then dipped in breadcrumbs and frozen. Fish fingers are known as a 'convenience food' because they are quick and easy to prepare.

15

DAIRY PRODUCTS

Milk has been part of our diet for centuries and we consume millions of litres of it every year. It is produced by all mammals, but we mostly use domesticated, vegetarian animals for milk. It is either drunk as it is or **processed** into dairy foods like cheese.

Cows

Cows are kept in dairy herds and milked every day. Milk used to be a common source of **bacteria**. Today, milk is heat-treated to kill germs and to make it safe to drink.

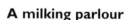

A milking parlour

Special cups gently squeeze the cow's milk from the udder into pipes. The pipes lead to a cold tank where the milk is kept fresh. It takes about ten minutes to milk a cow.

Camels

Milking a camel is quite a tricky job! Camels are easily annoyed and may bite or kick when they become angry. But their milk is rich in fat and protein.

Buffalo

In large parts of Asia and some parts of Africa, milk comes from buffalo. Their milk has more protein and fat than cows' milk.

Reindeer

In northern countries where it is very cold, reindeer are kept for their milk. Reindeer milk is much higher in fat and protein than any other milk.

Goats and sheep

Goats are kept in hilly areas and in deserts. They will eat almost anything – including brambles, shrubs and weeds. Goats' milk is often made into cheese.

Sheep are milked in Central Europe. Their milk is made into a distinctive tasting cheese. Pigs are not milked because it is difficult to milk a sow.

MILK PRODUCTS

*Milk contains a sugar called lactose which is easily changed into an acid by bacteria. This is called **souring** and causes the protein in milk to curdle. We use this natural change to make cheese and yoghourt.*

WHAT HAPPENS TO MILK

Most milk that we drink comes from cows. Different kinds of cows have been specially bred for their milk yield. Jersey cows, for example, produce milk which is very creamy and high in fat.

NUTRIENTS IN MILK

Milk consists mainly of water, with tiny droplets of fat dispersed in it. If unprocessed milk is left to stand, the fat rises to the top, and can be seen as the cream layer. Milk is a good food because it contains many nutrients.

Composition of milk	
Vitamins/Minerals	0.7%
Protein	3.3%
Fat	3.8%
Carbohydrate	4.7%
Water	87.5%

Cream

Cream is made by separating out the creamy part of milk. Nowadays this is normally done by machine. Double cream has a higher fat content (48%) than whipping (35%) or single (18%) cream.

Composition of cream	
Vitamins/Minerals	0.5%
Protein	1.5%
Fat	48%
Carbohydrate	2%
Water	48%

Butter

The traditional butter churn has now been replaced by a complex machine. This makes fat droplets in cream stick together to produce butter. Butter milk, a by-product, is drained away. The butter is then cut and wrapped in foil or waxed paper.

Composition of butter	
Vitamins/Minerals	1.5%
Protein	0.5%
Fat	83%
Water	15%

Yoghourt

Harmless bacteria in milk, called *lactobacilli*, are left to produce lactic acid at a warm temperature. This sours the milk, which then sets into yoghourt. Sugar or fruit are often added.

Composition of yoghourt	
Vitamins/Minerals	2%
Protein	5%
Fat	0.5%
Carbohydrate	12%
Water	80.5%

Wheat flour products

Wheat flour can be made into a huge number of foods – crackers, cakes, biscuits, puddings, pancakes, pastries and pies. The most important product though is bread. This is made from a dough of wheat flour, water and yeast. The dough is left in a warm place, so that the yeast can produce a gas which makes the dough rise. The dough can be made into hundreds of different shapes.

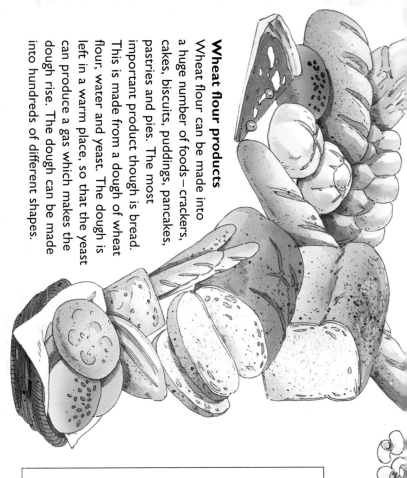

BREAD

This is an important food all around the world – it is even sometimes called 'the staff of life'. Different countries have their own special breads. From sandwiches to toast, bread is eaten at almost every meal.

Composition of bread	
Vitamins/Minerals	1%
Protein	9%
Fat	2%
Carbohydrate	42%
Water	38%
Fibre	8%

From the farm to your table

Cows are milked on the farm. The milk is then transported in a tanker to a processing plant.

Skimmed milk

All the fat (cream) is removed from the milk by machine. Skimmed milk is healthier than whole milk as it has less fat and fewer **calories**.

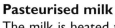

Pasteurised milk

The milk is heated to kill any harmful bacteria, and then cooled quickly.

Long life milk

The milk is heated to a very high temperature to kill all bacteria.

Dried milk

The milk is sprayed into hot air and dried into a powder. The powder is then sealed into an air tight container.

Evaporated milk

Some of the water is evaporated from heat-treated milk. It is then sealed into cans.

Condensed milk

This is like evaporated milk but with sugar added to make it thick.

The pasteurisation plant

Here the milk is heated to a temperature of 72°C for fifteen seconds and then rapidly cooled to 4°C. After strict tests for quality, the milk is poured into steam-cleaned bottles or cartons ready for delivery.

Cheese

Turning milk into cheese is a traditional way of preserving it. During this process, milk is allowed to become slightly sour. A special **enzyme** called rennet is added, and this 'sets' the milk proteins into thick curds. The liquid produced, called whey, is drained off, leaving the cheese to be salted and then packed into moulds to ripen. Cheeses are matured and flavoured in many different ways. Blue cheese has special types of harmless mould growing through it, which gives it the blue veins.

Composition of cheese	
Vitamins/Minerals	3%
Protein	26%
Fat	33%
Water	38%

FOOD FROM WHEAT

An ear of wheat

Wheat consists of grains, clustered at the top of a stalk.

It is surprising how many foods can be made out of wheat. Wheat is one of our most important cereal crops, and wheatfields can be seen in many areas of the world. The Prairies of America and the Steppes of Russia are important wheat growing areas.

Beard

A wheat grain

Inside a wheat grain is the wheat germ, which is rich in nutrients. The endosperm is the food store, and is mainly starch.

Wheat germ (a seed)

Endosperm (a food store)

Harvest time

A combine harvester picks the ears of wheat, then separates the grains from the stalks. Each grain is covered by a tough husk called the bran, which contains lots of fibre.

Actual size of wheat grain

Bran (a thick outer husk)

Milling of wheat

The wheat grains are torn open, then crushed and ground down into flour by mechanical rollers. Different types of flour can be made by sieving out coarser particles of bran.

Three main types of flour

Wholemeal flour

The whole wheat grain is used for this flour. It contains lots of fibre, and all nutrients from the grain.

Brown flour

Some of the bran layer (the fibre) is removed from the wheat grain during milling.

White flour

All the bran and the wheat germ are removed. Only the endosperm is used.

Pasta

Pasta is made out of flour from a special type of wheat known as durum wheat. This has a high protein content. Pasta is made into many shapes.

Cereals

Wheat can be made into breakfast cereals, which are a healthy food if the whole wheat grain is used. Cereals are often fortified with extra vitamins and minerals.

EGGS

We eat many kinds of birds' eggs – from tiny quails' eggs to huge ostrich eggs. All are rich in protein, vitamins and minerals, especially iron. The yolk of an egg is a food store, surrounded by a protective egg white and shell. The colour and shape of eggs vary from **species** to species and has nothing to do with the diet of the bird.

Quails' eggs   Hens' eggs   Ostrich egg

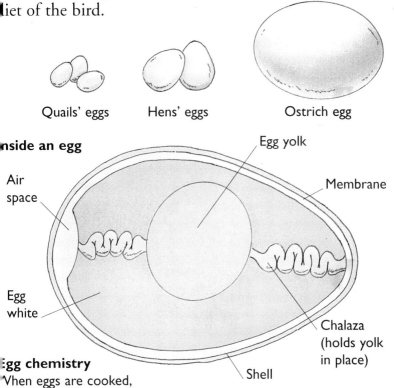

Inside an egg

Egg yolk

Air space

Membrane

Egg white

Chalaza (holds yolk in place)

Shell

Egg chemistry

When eggs are cooked, the proteins set or **coagulate**. By using different ingredients, or various methods of cooking, eggs are used in a huge variety of dishes throughout the world.

Eggs can go bad easily if they are not stored properly. The air space inside an egg grows bigger as an egg becomes older. This makes a fresh egg sink in water, but a stale egg will float! If eggs are really rotten, hydrogen sulphide gas is formed, which has a horrible smell.

COOKING FOOD

Some foods are eaten raw, such as carrots, lettuce and fruit, and in Japan many people enjoy raw fish. Other food needs to be cooked to soften it and make it easier to chew. Cooking also improves the taste of food and changes its shape and appearance. The heat of cooking kills bacteria, which could otherwise make us ill.

Cooking on an open fire
This is a traditional way of cooking and we still barbecue food in the same way. The heat from the fire cooks the outside of the food first. A spit is often used to rotate the food and so prevent burning in one place.

Frying
Batter, made from flour and water, can be cooked on a hot metal plate to make pancakes. We often use a frying pan to conduct heat into food. Besides pancakes, we fry many other foods like meat, fish and vegetables.

Cookers in kitchens

A modern cooker allows us to control heat. Hot air circulating inside an oven means that we can bake bread and cakes, or roast meat. We can also use the top of the cooker to boil, simmer, steam and fry food.

Microwave ovens

Microwaves penetrate food, giving energy to the food particles which generates heat quickly. Microwaves bounce off metal and so glass, china or plastic dishes are used in microwave ovens.

HERBS AND SPICES

Herbs are plants with sweet smelling leaves, like rosemary, mint, and basil. Some plants have seeds which are spicy and hot, like chili peppers.

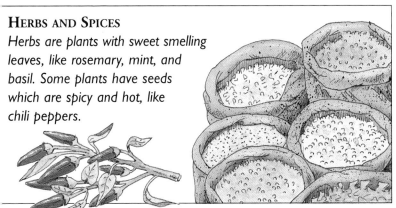

PRESERVING FOOD

Bacteria are microscopic living creatures that can be found all round us. They grow well in food, but can make the food rotten and poison us. There are many ways to prevent this from happening. Freezing, canning, pickling, drying and freeze-drying are some of the ways of preserving food.

Freezing

The temperature in a freezer is too cold for bacteria to grow and so we freeze food to keep it fresh for longer. Food is frozen quickly, usually with blasts of very cold air. Once frozen, food must be stored in a freezer at a temperature below -18°C.

Canning

The food is prepared and filled automatically into cans. The air at the top of the can is sucked out before the lid is sealed. The cans are then heated in a **sterilizer** to high temperatures to kill all bacteria. The food then lasts for years.

Pickling

Some foods, usually vegetables, are soaked in vinegar and then bottled in an airtight container. The vinegar an acid and this stops bacteria from growing, so the food is preserved. Eggs, onions and gherkins are popular pickled foods.

Drying

Bacteria cannot grow without water, so dried food lasts for a long time without going bad. In some countries, food is laid out to dry in the Sun – fish in China and fruits in the Philippines. More modern methods use hot air, generated in a factory, to **evaporate** water. Instant packaged potatoes and soups are produced in this way.

Freeze-drying

This method drys food quickly, making it porous and easy to **rehydrate** by adding water. Once fast-frozen, the food is put into a vacuum chamber. Here the ice crystals in the food change to steam, leaving the food dry.

LET'S CELEBRATE

Food is often served on special occasions. Holy days, weddings and birthdays are celebrated all over the world with a feast. These feasts can take a lot of preparation. For example, the Sardinian dish 'Cobbler's Bull' is roasted for several hours, in a deep ditch dug out of the ground.

Japan
At the New Year festival in Japan, many sorts of fish, simmered or fried, are served with vegetables, soya beans, seaweed rolls and rice.

Africa
A traditional West African celebration dish is a big casserole of chicken and beef with lots of rice and vegetables.

India
At an Indian wedding the main dish is semolina dough fried in balls and flavoured with sugar and saffron.

America
When Americans celebrate Thanksgiving, they eat roast turkey followed by pumpkin pie.

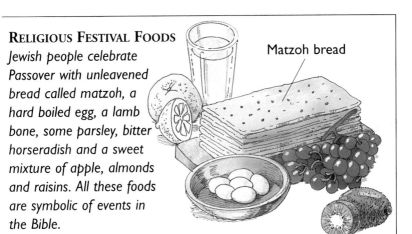

RELIGIOUS FESTIVAL FOODS

Jewish people celebrate Passover with unleavened bread called matzoh, a hard boiled egg, a lamb bone, some parsley, bitter horseradish and a sweet mixture of apple, almonds and raisins. All these foods are symbolic of events in the Bible.

Matzoh bread

Italy

'Cobbler's Bull' is served on special occasions in Sardinia, Italy. This dish is a hare stuffed inside a pig, stuffed inside a goat, stuffed inside a calf.

France

The centrepiece of a French wedding feast is often a huge pyramid of cream-filled profiteroles with caramel poured over. The pyramid can be a metre high.

Different kinds of bread

In Greece, at Easter, bread is baked into a variety of shapes and flavoured with cardamom seeds.

MARKETS AND SUPERMARKETS

There are lots of different ways of buying and selling food, and many kinds of food shops. Some sell only one kind of food – a baker sells bread and cakes. But other shops, like supermarkets, sell a wide variety of food.

Outdoor markets
There are outdoor markets in every country in the world where shoppers can choose from a wide selection of foods: fruit, vegetables, herbs, spices, and sometimes fish and meat too. The produce is always well displayed and very fresh.

Supermarkets
In a supermarket, most of the food is already weighed and packed in boxes, packets or jars. Carrots, for example, may be sold raw or canned or frozen. Supermarkets usually have a huge selection of different foods.

It is better to buy unprocessed foods because some packaged and tinned foods, though quick and easy to prepare, contain additives, like flavourings and colourings, and these can be harmful to our health.

The sell-by-date

Packets of food in a supermarket will have a date stamped on them. This will tell you if the contents are still fresh enough to eat.

BEST BEFORE END:
DEC 99

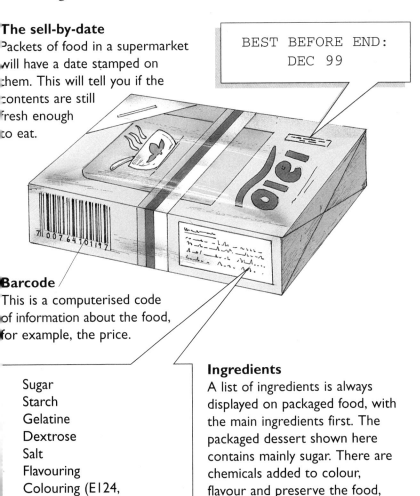

Barcode

This is a computerised code of information about the food, for example, the price.

Sugar
Starch
Gelatine
Dextrose
Salt
Flavouring
Colouring (E124, E102, E123)
Preservative (E220)

Ingredients

A list of ingredients is always displayed on packaged food, with the main ingredients first. The packaged dessert shown here contains mainly sugar. There are chemicals added to colour, flavour and preserve the food, and you should avoid too many of these.

FOOD FOR ALL

In some parts of the world there is hunger and **famine**. It may happen because of disasters like a drought or a flood. Poverty and wars are also causes of famine. Without food, children cannot grow properly and have no energy to move or resistance to disease. Adults also become ill and weak.

The importance of food

The child shown in the inset picture on the right is starving—little more than skin and bones, after a long time with hardly any food. The main picture shows the same child a few weeks after eating nourishing food, looking much healthier.

Scientists and farmers are working together to try to prevent famine. Improvements to water supplies and farming methods will help to prevent famine in the future. Farmers are now encouraged to use fertilizers and pesticides to help produce more crops. Also, new crops are being developed that are more resistant to drought and disease.

New crops

These are specially bred to give a higher yield of grain.

Maize

Rice

Wheat

Improved wheat

Improved maize

Improved rice

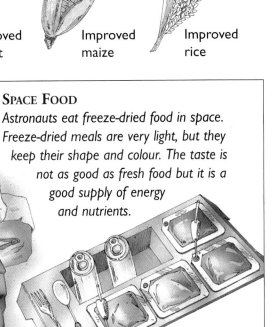

SPACE FOOD

Astronauts eat freeze-dried food in space. Freeze-dried meals are very light, but they keep their shape and colour. The taste is not as good as fresh food but it is a good supply of energy and nutrients.

AMAZING FOOD FACTS

● **Poisonous food** Some food contains natural poisons which can make us ill. In Japan, the liver of the puffer fish, a popular food, is highly poisonous and has to be cut out by specially trained people before the flesh of the fish is eaten.

● **Edible insects** Insects are a nutritious food and considered a delicacy in some countries. Ants and grasshoppers are popular in parts of South America, as are beetles in Asia. In Africa, insects are an important part of the daily, staple diet.

● **Cheese variety** France produces over 400 different kinds of cheese, including the famous ones such as Brie and Camembert. Britain, Holland, Denmark, Switzerland and America also have big cheese industries. Yet some countries eat very little cheese – the Chinese diet for example does not traditionally include dairy products.

● **Do carrots help us to see?** There is a saying that carrots help us to see in the dark. Carrots do contain plenty of vitamin A, which is needed for healthy eyes, but eating lots of carrots will not help us to see more clearly in the dark.

● **Soya beans** Soya beans are an amazing food as they have a huge variety of uses. These beans are very nutritious, and provide calcium, iron and B vitamins as well as having a higher protein content than most other foods.

● **Breakfast cereals** These are one of the few new foods. Breakfast cereal was invented in 1904 and has revolutionised our breakfast eating habits.

GLOSSARY

Bacteria Tiny forms of life that live all around us. They can make food go bad.

Breeding Choosing certain animals and plants which are stronger or better than others to go on to produce young.

Calories A measure of energy supplied by food.

Cereal A plant like wheat, whose seeds are used for food.

Coagulate The hardening of proteins when they are cooked.

Diet Food and drink that you eat regularly. Some people use 'diet' to mean that they are eating less to lose weight.

Energy You need energy to do everything, even sleeping.

Enzyme A protein that is produced by living cells.

Evaporate When water changes into steam, usually by being heated.

Famine When there is not enough food for people to eat.

Fibre A substance found in plants. It cannot be digested, but it is vital in our diet to help us to get rid of waste.

Grain The seeds of cereal crops such as wheat, corn, rice, barley and oats.

Nutrients Materials we obtain from food which are needed for our health. They are protein, carbohydrate, fat, vitamins and minerals.

Processed Food which is made in a factory. It often contains colourings and preservatives, to make it look more appealing and to last longer.

Rehydrate To restore water that has been lost when the food was dried.

Souring The change, caused by acids, that occurs in fresh milk after a few days.

Species A group of animals or plants which are alike in certain ways.

Sterilize To kill all the germs or bacteria in a food.

Tuber The short, thick part of some plant stems which grow underground. Potatoes are tubers.

Vitamins They are needed by your body to work smoothly.

INDEX *(Entries in **bold** *refer to an illustration)*